ADVANCE PRAISE

"Through his poetry, Bill Phillips reminds us of all that is beautiful
in our lives and the beauty with which God has surrounded us. If we
fail to pause in our daily lives to notice God's wondrous works, Bill
has done so for us, using words and imagery that reveal the glory of
God's design of man and of nature.

I pray Bill's work will inspire those who read it to come to the quiet
from time-to time, to seek the peace and contentment that can be
found in ourselves and to take stock of all that is beautiful and good
in our lives, as bestowed on us by God, the Architect of all Creation."

— Most Reverend William E. Lori, Archbishop of Baltimore

"Simple and profound, gentle and engaging, the poems of Bill
Phillips offer rich insights into life and nature. They are captivating
for those who love poetry and inviting to those who don't."

— Frank Nash SJ, Lemoyne University

"Thank you for sharing your poetry with me. It reflects your own
deep connection with the Lord. Your heart and grounded sensibil-
ities surface very readily in the metaphors and scenarios you share
with us in your poems."

— Bill Watters SJ, Pastor Emeritus, St Ignatius Baltimore

SILENT SPEAK

Poetry from Contemplative Living

SILENT SPEAK

Poetry from Contemplative Living

Bill Phillips Oblate, OSB

Apprentice House
Loyola University Maryland
Baltimore, Maryland

First Edition

Printed in the United States of America

Paperback ISBN: 978-1-62720-107-0
E-book ISBN: 978-1-62720-108-7

Design: Mary Del Plato
Editorial Development: Lorena Perez
Editing: Karl Dehmelt
Cover Photo: Cyndi Leigh at Cyndi Pachino Photography
        www.cyndipachinophotography.wordpress.com/
        cpachino@gmail.com

Published by Apprentice House

Apprentice House
Loyola University Maryland
4501 N. Charles Street
Baltimore, MD 21210
410.617.5265 • 410.617.2198 (fax)
www.ApprenticeHouse.com
info@ApprenticeHouse.com

Who to name without slighting some who have led me, pushed me, pulled me, all in the name of love that He commands of us? With His Grace and my wife Pat walking with me, these lines would not have seemed to flow from my pen unimpeded

TABLE OF CONTENTS

FOREWORD

Poets are the real seers in life. Through them we are able to gain a glimpse of the deeper truth and meaning of ordinary events. If we pay attention to them we will learn. If we are adventurous, we will follow them into the depths of their thoughts and find our edification in their verse.

This collection of poems contains a lifetime of adventure: sorrow, joy, curiosity, wins and losses are all present to one degree or another. In these "conversations" Bill Phillips bids us to stop and rest awhile as he shares with us his experiences of letting the silence of God speak to him. In this silent speech we are immersed in the love of God and our fellow man. God is always present to us. Our poet reminds us of this as he encourages us to talk to God. To spend time musing on God's blessings, so readily manifested in our lives – if only we will take the time to see them. Bill has taken the time to ponder these blessings in his life and to share them with us.

This collection comes from the heart. It is a collection of conversations with God, with the Master. If we are wise, we will take the time to read and meditate on these poems; to consider how we talk to God and engage with him in our daily lives.

We share a common humanity with the poet; our lives are bound together with his in our needs, success, and failures. Bill is a poet of beauty and resonance as it is found in the ordinary work-a-day world that we all inhabit. We find in these selections, a window into the spiritual life and energy of a man, a glimpse of his intimacy with God. So too, we find a mirror, which reflects an image of ourselves, of our own efforts to see God in all things and to reach a level of intimacy in which, through silent speak, we enter into our own conversation with the Master.

Kevin P. Shields
Farnham Way
Mays Chapel, MD

INTRODUCTION

It's hard to say when or if I laid these poems, stowed away somewhere in the deep mind where the practice of meditation and contemplation begin, fertilizing and energizing one's soul. I venture to guess blessings were given when I first recited 'Now I lay me down to sleep…' with my mother and father at the ripe age of two or three years old. Seeds were sown then that didn't bear fruit 'til I began the first of several journals in middle age.

When I began to review the journals it was apparent that God had been planning for me to write my thoughts down in poetic form not only from what had triggered the prose style in the first place, but what was presently going through my soul from day to day experiences. He seemed to be the ink in my pen, flowing out into my words; all He required from me was to neatly write out His urgings. I have never been more joyful since.

It's my idea not to title my poems but rather for the reader do their own titling. I venture that perhaps He might bless you too and you'll start to see Him in your daily living as you gradually fall in love with Him. Jot your thoughts down. Don't wait 'til later, they seem to slip away.

As Pedro Aruppe SJ * wrote :

Falling in Love with God

"Nothing is more practical than finding God,
that is, than falling in love in a quite absolute,
final way. What you're in love with, what
seizes your imagination, will affect everything.
It will decide what will get you out of bed in the

morning, what you'll do with your evenings,
how you will spend your weekends, what you read,
who you know, what breaks your heart, and what
amazes you with joy and gratitude. Fall in love,
stay in love, and it will decide everything."

Pedro de Aruppe Y Gondra,
28th Superior General of The Jesuit Order,
b.1907-d. 1991

DARK WITH EARLY MORN

Even though it's dark with early morn
the birds are singing their wake up calls.
The sun is quietly creeping through trees,
upper boughs waving with Your presence,
longing to share Your spirit with us.

**

The classroom walls covered with
water color art, expressions of
adolescent wonders
How would the artists words describe
the meanings hidden there?

**

Each unborn child has stories to tell
from seeds growing in their souls
cast there in mothers wombs,
if only we'd allow them life to share.

**

What tree will be drawn or smiling
flower face exposed that talks to
innocent young minds unburdened
by trash that we adults collect.

**

Evil lurks looking for sustenance
as we eagerly feed the beast
trading our souls for emptiness,
exchanging blessings eternal
for temporary rushes that soon
drift off and leave us in our doom.

**

Though times change we remain
as lost children peering hungrily at
penny candy that has lost its sweetness
to be swallowed up by anxious hearts
that only He can satisfy.

**

My soul needs R&R, rid of hustlers
and hawkers selling nightly news
same old twists painted over
like next years cars each segment
with hot anchors and token others
starched hair and sassy smiles
weather, sports, and latest shootings
satisfying appetites.

**

The Cantors voice overwhelmed
the Liturgy, a shade off key, though she meant well.

**

Baltimore is bleeding, evil works
the street, brothers and sisters
besieged, no relief in sight
though prayers are offered.

**

Empting my soul of me
and old gods leaves room
for The Divine to curl up
and rest awhile.

**

Help me to accept the oddities
of my fellows and hopefully
they'll overlook mine.

**

Brave men and women dressed in white
and blue in open view hoping to calm
the streets so they too can sit with kin
and live another day with loved ones round.

**

Lord, let me see you in each day
not looking for ever new things
but to love you more deeply in
gifts already given, my church,
family, work, friends, the world
round me, always aware of your
Beauty, grandeur, and mercy.

**

Every day brings new routes to follow
Emmaus Road with ever more strangers,
Could some be angels in disguise testing
how we worked the field that day
so be alert and ready surely mixed
among us could be Christ the King.

**

On my journey, how far am I to go,
what share of joy and sorrow,
how many falls to rise from
what part of me be you,
how many smiles and tears to share
with poor and needy ones.

**

God is not a concept nor paradigm,
All in All, Word, Love, Mercy,
His creation from dust and dirt
He made us, His grass, trees, sea,
the air we breath, His Son, His Mom,
His Saints and rascals alike,
His you, His me.
We forget to thank Him
for His generosity.

**

Absorption in the world is our bane.
The Lord was asked what is the greatest commandment
He gave three answers, Love God, neighbor and self.
to do the first and second, we must be doing self
if we don't accept the truth of who we are then how
can we expect to know how to love Him, by what
measurement are we to use if we can't admit our sin
am I lovable in the first place, worthy of His gift?

**

How much Christ is in me or of me?
if I met me would I love me?
He loves all us unconditionally,
good or bad, worthy or not
no adjectives attached,
just my humanness.

**

Save me Lord from myself
open my eyes and heart to
Your ways
Don't let me strut about
like a bird flashing its feathers.

**

When you sit in silence is
your phone or pad so much
a part of you that you
can't spare some time
away from them for
The Beloved?

**

The summers brought more rain than usual
grasses, plants , and trees still carry green
long past the usual browning season of Augusts known
perhaps He's making ready for winter woes to come.

**

She hadn't ' been to Mass in a couple months, too boring',
After we prayed and held hands, she received the Eucharist
it appeared to light a spark, ever so slightly,
perhaps the glow will blossom into a new beginning.

**

Keep me on the straight and narrow,
crooked or wide, which ever You chose
help me to follow the paths You pick
not to fall off with my impatience and greed.

**

From whence I came from mothers womb,
scarcely have I loved You in return

**

Let me be wise that I may see the road to follow
Not to darkness but to light, lit by Your lovers
Your chosen ones of all stripes, Desert Fathers,
corner beggars, mystics, martyrs, Saints
and sinners alike who went before me.

**

The king prepared his feast but guests reniged
with other plans to do.
Standards eased so idlers could attend,
one arriving with soiled garments and stubbled chin
only to be cast outside for disrespecting the host.

**

The trash truck pulled across the road, two souls clinging aft,
Would it be fair to call them trash or refuse men?
Ecology conscious, dutifully collecting,
why not just call them humans and drop the adjectives,
we like to separate ourselves with tags, black or white,
African or oriental, fat or lean, gay or straight, man or women.
He knows us merely as human, no description added.
All He asks is 'Do you love me, and your neighbor as yourself?'
no other categories weigh as much, such as man has made.

**

On the road to Emmaus allow me
to love even the bumper huggers
who wish to push on past.

**

Altar flowers always seem
to be looking up to You, smiling
If only the down trodden could
do the same.

**

May You run to me as if I were a stranger
returning home from lost and lonely climbs
like once the prodigal son.

**

Forgive me Lord for what
I haven't done that You
had planned, a waste of gifts
given, meant for me to do.

**

There are those who've asked
and some who haven't who
need a prayer of petition,
afraid to ask the Sheppard
waiting for His lost sheep.

**

Though 93 with parts a wear
and tubes that help him breathe
his chair has wheels but his eyes
still spark and lips that smile
accepting Holy gifts.

**

Fall flowers wait their turn to display Your beauty
Trees impatient holding back their glory
as if there's competition among each leaf.

**

What new surprises wait for me
that I pass up each day
consumed with hopelessness?

**

You've prepared creation to be meted out
at your command if only we'd be patient

**

We don't deserve or earn Your love
but it's there for the taking.

**

What's its name, the one
you spend most time with?
the one you press your ear to
or look lovingly into its face?
Does it have eyes to meet,
does your pulse race when
given so much love?
Of course its your best friend
you say, somewhat like your pet
Does it cuddle up on wintry nights,
how's its cooking skills,
does it help you with the chores?
If I were as close to my phone I'd
name it so I could introduce it round.

**

Lord, let me share the gifts
you give with all I meet this day
whether those I see the same
each morn or others first time by.

**

We/re having an unusually hot summer
perhaps there's something to this warming thing
that pols and pundits blame on humans.
This winters said be like last,
the winter fairy has a hand to play.

**

Now that summers blooms and blossoms
had their turn, make way for falls display
waiting in the wings.

**

The me generation has it's selfies
Me first seems to be the trend
I wonder if they see their splinters
disguising what the real me that hides there.

**

The morning walk was holiday quiet
souls still sleeping off yesterdays
the sun had not reached the upper branches
no birds singing or frogs a croaking.
even crows had little to caw about
it seems I'm the only guest in God's beauty.

**

The trees are silent as if waiting
for marching orders, each with
a time to shed their summer glory
I wonder which will be the color champ
It seems the winner shifts among the soft wood.

**

A crow announced it's presence
calling signals to it's kin
I wonder what the crows are saying.
some secret caw code I'm sure

**

A single dove lights quietly above
Where's it's mate who usually tags along?
Is it old and widowed or some young
buck looking for a bride?

**

Even the quiet is quiet
only disturbed by beetle noise
and hum of tires racing by.

**

Saint Benedict teaches that talking
a good game is not enough
Christ is waiting and wanting
for us to show what we have to give.

**

Modern man has apps and software
to keep on top of things in place
of spiritual direction badly needed
websites are our tutors, able to
take over Holy Roles
One wise Priest friend spoofed
that if Christ asked today "Who do they
say I am?" We could always ask 'Google"

**

Oh to do as Mary did,
a first time mother,
filling her term just
as The Father asked.

**

We pray that all
first time moms,
married or no,
follow Mary's way
and answer Yes!

**

What's its name, the one
you spend most time with,
Is it potty trained, does it
need a baby sitter, or is it
just the latest gizmo some new
billionaire has thought up?

**

Lord, give me the will and
energy in searching for You.
You are indeed the Light,
lead me from my darkness.

**

Lord, in my daily round
Let me speak no deceit
Let me love all and what
You have created.

**

Labor Day and roads still bare
most milking last minutes
for their stay to miss long
backups at the Bay Bridge.

**

They're marvels, some of
The Masters finest work
Their daughter called to sit
 beside Him sooner than most
His plan for her complete
She lives on in her parents manner
strong in faith and love like her,
a witness to His wonderment

                              **

We are all children
returning to small things,
like playing games that
give Him joy, games not
so serious, loose held
like little friends with
runny noses crowding
up to a penny candy counter.

                              **

When lies we've stored are
exposed to light and truth
beauty rises out of darkness.
long lying mistakes unresolved.
We seemed to love our hates
we've stored, mostly long
forgotten how they got there,
evil got its way.

                              **

Silence allows us to slow,
to see beauty that we passed
when noise was our companion.
to busy tending phones and pads,
clamor ruling, stored and filed
for future uses biasing our
hearts, prejudicing our souls.

                              **

Silent souls seem to
see His Beauty for
the first time, again,
passing as strangers,
hidden there.

**

Silence allows one to be all things,
both liberal and conservative,
living in paradox peacefully,
His Beauty in array, nothing lost.

**

Apps allow for endless knowledge,
Wisdom suffers through a lifetime,
Only silence gives it's bounty
honed from our journeys
The Master in the lead.

**

Morning walk in hazy humidity,
filtered sunlight, people out
for different reasons, a schoolgirl,
head down, backpack weighting,
straightaway facing, eyes a wonder,
my hello brings up her chin with
eyes now smiling, one of His lambs.

**

People pass with measured strides,
just men and women to describe
no adjectives to lay on them,
no mind benders to clutter things.
no nationality or party affiliation,
no gender stamp or sexual preference
just man and women like God named

**

Spiritual journeys are quite apart,
each driven by Gospel light,
straight from the Fathers mouth,
with stand-in others, saints and
prophets guiding, words spoken
once, unchanged over time.

**

The Chapel smells fresh and clean
As if expecting guests to call.
One other soul stands his hourly watch,
the only sound a rush of AC air.
It's wonderful to be alone with You
although I'd wager it'd please You best
if more looked up at You.

**

The Eucharist, a gift offered to sick
souls, tired from hospital routines,
night nurse calls interrupting sleep,
in others pain has robbed
them of rest, can I be Your proxy,
or dare I wake them?

**

Without silence how can we hear His Beauty?
We seem to gather and store our noise in
memory banks destined to play it's role
when least expected, drowning our peace.

**

My noise is unique, different than any others.
we guard our noise as if it's treasure,
hidden in a secret place, defining us.

UNKNOWING

How's your silence today
where you encounter Him
who waits and watches,
mercy and compassion
in abundance?

❋❋

What matter of ways is this
that flows from my pen?
Nothing I have seen or heard
firsthand is subject here.

❋❋

The whole of it will never be known
for what measures whole in infinity or eternity.

❋❋

You prepared this day for all of us.
Let me not ignore my place in it,
To give your Love away freely.

❋❋

We must schedule quiet time
much as we do meal times
and visits to the gym.

Does daytime TV drama describe
who I am or have become?
What part do I play with my life
that helps to distain the evils lurking
waiting to welcome any soul who dallies,
evil's legions are never sleeping,
all are subject to their luring.

**

Lord, keep me from being of a double heart and soul
some for You and some for the evil one.
Help me live in humility, recognizing my weaknesses,
to become fully human, fully divine, as Your Son is.

**

At first it's hard to do, other obligations seem
to take priority squeezing out good intentions.

**

It's best to become as a child again,
pure in spirit, not trapped by the
evil one in worldly fancies.

**

Seldom on our journeys do we go so straight
that cruise control or auto pilot leads us home
We're prone to take back roads in our confusion
losing our way, detouring our plans, we're lost.

**

Many times we find we've lost our way,
interruptions plague our progress,
serenity is hard to come by, dryness rules,
I need to reset, much like my bulky computer.

**

Noise is ever in our midst, waiting,
rhythmic, beating as if a drum,
flashes, sparks, squeaks leaking out
of shells looking for attention.

**

It's easier making noise than quiet,
how does one manage stilling
demons looking for weak souls?
Demon noise gathered from life's
rubbings and heart aches,
prejudices we hate to give up,
though we know we should.

**

Once quiet becomes priority
one must fix a time to meet
much like a guest expected.

**

When shall we meet, morn or eve,
how many times a day or
are we talking weeks or years?

**

If diligence takes over, one begins to change,
mellowing, becoming more like Him
who waits patiently for us, in darkness.

**

Don't fret when missing schedules'
He's always joyful, waiting
for a lamb who's headed home.

**

One day the blissful happens in quiet,
sensing He's there,
perhaps a flash or spark appears
though fast it's flown again.

**

Even though in traces
you'll long for such
Beholding times again.

**

You pine to tell others
the Joy to share,
but explaining is fruitless,
He decides when and where.

**

What noises occupy the soul?
each has their own that define
the depth and width of unknowing.

**

We pass by each other deep inside our shell
pent there in self consciousness, glued
to who we think we are, hard letting go
as if I meant an hello.

**

Say Hi to passers by and watch surprise that wells up,
most have startled smiles to exchange,
others won't let go as if to like their loneliness.

**

When I look for your will and follow it
worries are dampened and paths open unclogged.

**

Old friends distilled from spiritual encounters
are called before our time.
Will they pray for us
who are still on travels home?

**

Forgive my dust I've caused
let me bath your feet and
take me back again.

**

In noiseless silence
I know you're there
even in my rawness.

**

We only experience God in
Unknowing even then He seems
to enjoy the hidden role in darkness.

**

Inner silence is not measurable,
much like infinity,
no limits, no containment.

**

We know the noises that interrupt our silence
like sins, we seem to like our choices.

**

I guess there's someone scientific working on eternity,
when it begins and ends, and when each becomes a part.

**

Are we each planned for our own space in time?
God has His plan for each just as He
asked Mary to carry the Christ child.
He didn't mean she should only tote the
Babe until He birthed but rather for
all His human time allotted 'til His agony.
God meant from first the cells began to grow
within the Virgin womb, the Son's humanity
multiplying, much the same for us as we first grew,
and much the same as our humanity began,
in our mothers womb, much the same for each
aborted soul slaughtered, not to fulfill His plan.

**

HOSPITAL VISITS

Lord help me to help them
I bring Your body to sustain them
how will they welcome You?
Will it be with a smile or a tear,
I pray it's not a no.
We bring your body to these sick rooms
yet some deny You and wary You
Call me to be your Simon
and bare the weight away.

**

What measure does He use for graces given,
Do all the yes's weigh the same to Him?
Do visits to the sick or patience with our fellows
balance scales like Mary's yes did then?

**

Eyes ask what's he want from me?
Smiles tell me 'Thanks' when
offered Holy Gifts.

**

She was sitting up, mute, a tube about her throat
We prayed together, I used words, she tears,
she clutched my hands in silence, love exchanged.
Most encounters are calm, smiles in place of tears,
Painless eyes offering thanks, blessings reward.
The haunting faces linger after, I can't forget them,
just as You've remembered me.

**

The Host remains in darkness as faith draws me within.
Perhaps my knock is weak, I'll try harder then.
I know my garments dirty and I really need a shave
I question if I'd answered too, if I showed up for Him.
It's wonderment He waits this long for return on graces given,
Has he left me time on earth to return the love I'm loaned?
Some are offered suffering as a wake up
call from the Beloved, a sentinel reminding
us that our earthly time is drawing ever shorter,
We must discern Your will and be alert,
suffering may be the sign He has prepared for us.

**

She was lying in an Intensive Care Unit
The left side of her face raw with burns,
An eye sealed shut, a shriveled ear, no hair;
We prayed, I offered her the Eucharist
A tear flowed from her opened eye
that looked away self-consciously
I asked her to look at me
my tears, mixed with hers
brought a smile from her
Exchanged love that He
had shared with us.

**

At hospital our plan was to bring His body there,
a visit that would bring our souls along,
graces to be exchanged.
Your plan wasn't ours, icy roads prohibited visits
A simple fact was learned, the shots are Yours to call
and we are left to pray for those whose
names were only known by You that day.

**

A patient, wearing a ventilator,
precious oxygen helping to heal.
A visitor was sitting with her and accepted
His body for her, graces shared
We began the 'Our Father', she in Spanish
confusing me. I held my words letting
her lead the prayer in native tongue.
When finished, we chatted.
The patient, a Nun, served the visitor's
village for many years, sowing seeds
that bared fruit that day for each of us.

**

I made my usual rounds calling on
the sick and broken but I did not
recognize Your face in them.
Was it me who didn't look for you
or were You hiding there all along?
I have no right to think You're waiting
for me though I am sick and broken too.

**

She was out of her room in therapy,
I found her there, a therapist beckoned,
She wondered who I was, what I
wanted, her face frozen, apprehensive.
Would you like to receive the Eucharist?
Hesitantly came an 'alright'.
She received, I recited the Assisi prayer,
her face melted into a smile
We exchanged spiritual love
given to each by the Beloved.

**

IT SEEMS YOU CONCEAL YOURSELF

It seems you conceal yourself
but then invite us to find you
like children playing hide and seek.
in your hidden-ness we must always
seek you if we are to find you.
Blindness and certitude are found
in search of you who tantalizes,
but then again retreats into
darkness and wonderment.

**

We don't visit Him as if He were
a natural wonder like Niagara Falls.
How do you visit a darkness hiding in
your soul or passing by in the wind?
We don't know what we're looking for
except words we've put to beauty or His body
waiting for us in a Chapel Monstrance.

**

If perchance I stand before You face to face
protect me Lord, lest I melt like wax beneath Your feet.

**

He died for us in His passion and
now desires us to seek Him in ours.
Is it unworthiness that causes
your darkened presence?
Will we see you face to face or
will we fade and wilt in your
radiance and beauty?

**

Scars remain where once a virgin
soul was born.
No longer pure when seeds were sown.
Now rocks and weeds are strewn
where once you hid, waiting for me.

**

Light of love. probe my soul, drive
out lingering darkness
Lead me back to Jerusalem to the
hill of shame where I can meditate
on your love and light.
Forgive my sins and lies that nail
you back to the tree.
Turn on your light so I can see
you sitting in the pews all 'round me.

**

Good Shepard, your lambs have strayed
down into the deep gullies and washes,
down where wolves wait hungry.
You hurry after them, your sashes flying,
you're willing to die for them, even hanging on a tree.
What price to pay for wanderers such as we,
We'll be off again and you'll be right behind
to anoint our heads and overflow our cups.

**

Our prodigal sons and daughters, sisters
and brothers, how do we welcome their return?
What inheritance have we left them to help
them deal with our tarnished world, the
many pigsties to work and corn husks to eat?
I see many of them coming down the road, let
us welcome them home with God like love that
was denied them in their youth while we pursued
our fortunes of folly.
After all, we were told the future was plastics.

**

Silence and solitude suffer from the mechanical
and technical onslaught of the latest electronic must-haves.
We no longer listen to our inner voices but prefer the
persistent clamor of hawkers.

**

No one shares our silent place
where I hope to meet You, a place
where our words are never given away.
where mostly I listen more than speak,
for what am I to say that You don't already know?

**

Oh precious silence when candles
die and voices fade away,
the Mass is over but You remain
hidden in darkness behind
the Tabernacle door.
It's time to leave and find You waiting
on the street.
I know you're there in eyes that
weep for love.
I search for you in others eyes and
mostly find you there exchanged.

**

The contemplative life leads us deeper
into the mystery of God
As we plunge deeper into the mystery
we come to know less about Him
whom we are seeking.
We never arrive closer to answers,
only that we come up with more questions.
The intellect starves as faith fattens on the mystery.

**

How to hate mothers and fathers
yet love our neighbors as ourselves,
Or how to hate anyone when You
are there within them.
I have come to think in unknowings
in order to know You.
Less intellect leads to deeper faith;
there is no fullness without prior emptiness,
how is it that the less I know of You
the more I want to know
the more I perceive of you the more
I pine to see You in your fullness?
Forgive my sins that stand in place of You.
In silence before the Monstrance
nothing needs to be said.
The only words needed in silence are
words to explain the rush in one's soul
when He decides to visit.

**

Oh chapels' banging door and furnace fan,
creaking hinge, you break the spell.
Call me back to You.

**

Why must I weary You and cause
You to search for me in wilderness
and unswept floors?

**

Knowledge of God does not come from reading
or seeing, for what is His shape, how do you draw
up something with no beginning and no ending, eternal?
What does God weigh if in fact does weight share some
part of His nature?
Does He have a scent about Him, what colors make
up the whole? He doesn't answer to any of man's criteria.
Though we can't see Him, He watches us, inviting us to
be with Him, not in mans made-up words, but rather the
speak of silence that holds His mystery.

**

It's middle fall and semi-darkness, Mass is calling.
Some cars, Paul's and Phil's and Frank's.
They have their spot along with the silent one
who leaves early for work.
I know most all by name if not by back of heads.
Some kneel, some sit, some slouch in silent conversations;
What brings them here each day like me?
It's not for me to know, those also in search of the mystery
fully revealed. I offer prayers for what they pray for.
Like me, can they discern His will that He has planned for them?.

**

I merit no special grace nor have I earned a small glimpse of You;
In this life I'm destined to know You only in darkness and silence,
And that's enough for now.

**

The Divine Master possesses all things in creation and
shares all of it in love with his laborers in the field.
We are not to pick and choose among His gifts like children in
a candy store, nor pout and stomp our feet when others have more
    toys.
We are not to nibble at others goods as if we deserved a share,
If we accept His gifts and offer them to others who are without,
we do His will and please Him in return.

**

The Gettysburg battlefield still holds the
ghosts of those who dueled there,
brothers stalked and sniped there,
still unclaimed bones lie amid the earth
and stones that haven't told their stories yet.
They still cry out to us for help and understanding.
They marched in lines abreast, straight, broken only
by cannon and rifle fire, blood belching, bones crushed,
parts of men, arms and legs still wrapped with uniforms
in place, among what's left of them.
Warfare goes on but now includes our sisters, part of the carnage
We haven't figured out peace yet, it'll be the death of us.

**

She was sitting up, mute, a tube about her throat.
We prayed together, I used words, she tears,
and clutched my hands in silence, love exchanged.
Most encounters are calm, smiles in place of tears,
Painless eyes offering thanks, blessings reward.
The haunting faces linger after, I can't forget them,
just as You remember me.

**

Oh Perfect Sacrifice, what little we in turn
Give back to you in love that your desire.
I can't contain your beauty or your breath,
The pursuit is never ending, but your promise drives me on.

**

This wall, these windows, the altar, flowers, Tabernacle,
candles, the remaining souls in pews about.
You're everywhere, in sunlight steaming in, the
very life you give to breath, I need not search afar.

**

Oh Timeless One, another day you've
given me to live and seek and love.
What again will I complicate, when plain
it's me You seek?

**

Lord, your seeds are everywhere.
How do I know which are mine?
Others have gifts that You have sown,
let me know and care and cultivate my own.
There is no easy way to reach Him,
No magic pill, no app, no need of further
search, ancient is enough.
But no less demanding, we must rid ourselves of us
and sit before The King without our clothes.

**

We have Silent Speak that's secret, only to You and me.
No mortal ears to hear, not Popes or Saints or Kings,
They know not what we say, these pearls of love we share.

**

This life, this world, this very day would
be naught, save faith and prayer in You.
Who could we believe in or petition for our needs?
My step outside my door each day would lack
it's wonder, the road to my Emmaus would not
include other journeymen
The Church would be darkened, no others,
No Mass to glory in.
You wouldn't be there to welcome me in Love.

**

The more I come to know You through
your grace, the more I want to know.
The more I come to know You through
your grace the more I know I don't know.
Keep me simple Lord, not haughty.
I'm not sure footed with the lofty.
My place is with the poor and simple
ones like me.
Silence, no words, no thoughts,
just dark space, quiet peace.
The Beloved waits, longing for a visit.
He doesn't wait for words or warpage,
 listening He's prepared.
As faith deepens, I welcome the desert
where we can visit there.
Though you're unseen, I know to flee
into your arms there and rest in Mystery.
The evil one knows he's not welcome in
our desert, and we can shun him there.
I know You don't need my words
so I sit in silence, listening.
Though I find You in silence and solitude
I pray I don't overlook your presence in all
the noise and clutter we have made
of Your creation.

**

The King stoops down to the beggar
and begs him to be King.
Lord draw me to You in the smile of a little child
And the memory ridden eyes of the lonely widow.
Lord, forgive our barbarity that dishonors you,
no matter what path we follow, if in battle or
clinic, in foreign lands or at home, as we steal
Your gift of soul to humankind and shed our
Brothers' blood.
a life planned ahead, evil has destroyed again.
a severed head, a fetus bagged to throw away,
an urban corner claims its quota, the school yards suffer same.
What has man become, or has he always been this way?
Have we been spared these horrors 'til Twitter and Facebook
brought us up to speed?

**

St Anthony's Shrine, such peace and beauty here.
There is no noise 'cept water trickling from a spout.
It's peaceful being alone with You, but there,
a distant plane drones on.
We converse in silence, only nature's noises interrupt.
It is You who speaks in tongues of silent breath, no
words are needed when wonder says it all.
The wind announces Your presence, although I see
You in waving trees amongst the gardens.
Are you in the trickle of the fountain?
Some of Your beauty has peaked in the plants and
flowers that have shown their best since buds of spring.
We mourn their death, too bad we failed to look upon
their full blown season, their rest is coming soon enough,
when all their dressings fall and wither, snow bound.
We'll pass the winter beauty only to miss spring's call to
watch in wonder Your beauty burst forth again, unnoticed.

**

Evil thrives in many forms and we all feed the pot.
Make this a day that I stand up and stare the beast away.
Another day in Jerusalem when You were slain in hate.
Christ weeps again to see his kin shed their blood for Him.
More martyrs are at the gate, pray hurry let them in.

**

My terror came, it crept up behind, and I was trapped and walled.
But in Your love that lavished there You saved me as you planned.
What's left for me is I discern to mimic what you've shown,
To look in eyes that cry as I when You lifted me to You.
Let me search for sheep and give to them the love You gave to me
There names are 'Lovely Lady' and 'Gentle Man', all those I see
    each day.
A trade: I'll give away the love exchanged for the love you've
    loaned to me.

**

There are days when Silent Speak is interrupted
by demon speak, when interlopers push their
way out of the darkness and point their fingers
at me and tell Him what a hypocrite I am.

**

'Do with me what You will'…do I really mean it,
 am I ready to become poorer, to give away all that is not You?
Without knowing what You might do with me,
when will I know You're through,
will this entail a lifetime?

**

I wish there was a pattern to His visits,
But He doesn't play that way.
We must be open to His dropping by
when least expected.

**

The chapel's neatly kept, the Monstrance beckoning.
Peace is palpable, interrupted only by sinful callers.
As I sit before the Monstrance. I wonder what He sees in me.
In soul silence different guests arrive who interrupt the peace
and mostly interfere and block His view of me.
The Master knows them well, they've pried and pried before;
There's no rush, no competition or timing, You'll find me
when you're ready, keep me alert, simple and poor in spirit.
I often fail to find you in haughty places.
Why do I surf the internet or seek in the media when
I know it's fruitless finding you there in your majesty?

**

It's quiet, only early souls are here
A distant voice is out beyond the door.
It's one of us who comes with wife in tow.
She's sweet and smiles but never kneels or
walks the aisle to bliss and beauty, the Eucharist.
When Mass concludes, he leads her out to home
with her smile in place.

**

In silence we pray to Him and if no answer comes,
take heart, He loves our desire to be with Him,
even though He remains in darkness and mystery.
'The Word became flesh'…then His body became bread,
His blood wine; will we ever understand such love as this?

**

Who knows but You what tugs at our souls,
what interrupts our peace, what separates us from You?

**

I marvel as the early's adore You in silence
It lifts my soul with them.
Wordless praise, what glories pass their tongues?
You listen to them all.
The 'fronts' and 'backs' have all arrived
They seem to save the middle pews for 'later' souls
who hire to the harvest too, their wages same as ours,
no need to measure them.
The Mass is done, and each soul has their parting,
some rush out to fill a schedule self imposed,
others talk aloud about last night's win or loss.
Some leaving seem to sense that quiet worked for them,
a small and dwindling few need more time and so remain
in silence alone with Him.
As we leave the Holy place we must remember to take our
souls along, His sheep await us to help them home again.

**

I pray for the Church, your Priests and Deacons that
welcome your Church, External, your Marthas.
The envy is with the better part, Your Mary's
the Church, Silent, where You share secrets that
grow from mustard seeds.
I know you'll be happy if I give away today all that You
gave me yesterday, and I'll be happy to receive whatever
You Grace me with today.
There's consolation in knowing that You have infinite love
for such as me, no bind of measure in infinite things.
So why do I worry if You will have mercy on me today
 as You had on me yesterday?

**

In silence You seem to have fled and left me
is it that You have tired of my stumbling,
that I haven't discerned your plans for me?
Give me courage to see what You ask of me
or what it is I have become that displeases You.
Watch and wait the scriptures tell us.
I have found that You like me to seek and find.
The light of day exposes You to me in
others that I meet along the way.

**

Help me to overcome self today in all I do,
In all I see, in all I meet, in all I love
as if it's the first time we've met.
May I live and love in truth of whom and what I am
and how little that becomes when excluding You.
Though You are unknown in darkness,
Your presence is palpable when sitting in pew,
silent with other pilgrims.
Prayer's arrive and sit in their private pew
space like pieces fitting in a puzzle.

**

In silent morn, in darkness and mystery, my soul searches
never to glimpse the un-glimpse-able, never to contain the
un-contain-able, only to be left to un-know You again.
You choose to allow me a glimpse of You contained in
the pleading eyes of Your poor.
Would I go on searching, if in fact You
allowed me once a glimpse of your beauty?
I pray I'll claw and climb to see You one day in full.

**

Now I lay me down to sleep…I prayed as a child,
on my knees, hands clasped skyward, eyes closed.
My mom and dad teaching me to love as only a child loves,
    unconditionally.
As I grew up and older, the world took over, guiding me,
    persuading,
pushing, shoving, luring, some truth, lots of trash.
Lost steps, lost family, lost job, lonely of lonely days on 'the farm'.
Weeks, months, total despair! Lost faith, slipping down the
    mountain.
I pine for those 'Lay me down days'.

**

Sundays alone were the worst, Sunday papers fully read only filled
    the morning.
I only owned a bike, getting around took up more time, breakfast
    time,
ride out time, any road, just take out time.
Heading home, a 2 roomer, but what I owned fit.
It's Fathers Day, or Thanksgiving, or Christmas, holidays alone
    are frightful,
I lost control, maybe a phone call, none this time, maybe next.
This dark hell is overwhelming, pile things up, light the match,
give the bike away, on a train out.
Time runs out, I can't cope! God, help me, you're my only guest.

**

Your legions are arriving, each peers to see who shares
the pews, are they regulars or is that some new one there?
Heads down or up, some frowns and smiles mix.
It's a comfort to the regulars to see new faces there,
'cause we know it pleases Him who comes to visit too.

**

This day begins in thanksgivings, where do we begin?
From Your first gifts to us? That's a start.
But how does one count the beach-sands or the
waves that pound them there?
We overlook most blessings, forgive me Lord
that I withhold my love in thanks-giving..

**

Help us to become like little birds
that peck and peck shells to free and fly.
That we might learn to fly our way
to you as you willed for us to do.

**

Why not be born in a stable where the poor and animals live
after all, his mom was a peasant girl and his step dad a tradesman.
His mission was to die and save the lowly and the poor,
not just the Kings who humbled themselves to offer first gifts.
Strips of cloth were manger wear for the Son of God,
Who arrived in Bethlehem in His naked humanity,
no in-laws to gift a crib or car-seat.
The Christ child left in Mary's arms on donkey back
towed toward Egypt by Joseph to escape the crazy king.

**

How can there be unbelievers when man carves
wood that makes music sound like angel voices?
We forget Him who made the tree.
What about the Doctors who mend the
shattered bones or parts eaten by disease?
Surely something great made the bone that wasn't working.
What lab helped out, what person came up with plans?
And who followed up with tools and such to fix it right again?
The nurse, aides, and healers that share Gods secret ways

**

How can we forget You when You are Yourself
the day, just to have another chance to breath it in?
To see your beauty on display, the sky, the seas,
the growing things, the flowers and the trees,
so much we haven't logged yet or given names to call.
All these gifts packaged in man's humanity that we've
wasted, ignored in each others gifts we fail to share.

**

Beautiful rose, God created your face
And thorns to protect your majesty.
Our soul's the same but we are weak
we lose our duel with hate.

**

In the quiet of the chapel
You plant your seeds in silence.
Other pilgrims come and go.
It's winter, the air filled with
furnace noise and coughs,
A soul comes in breathless distress.

**

The Virgin was called and gave a Yes
to grow the Christ bound by her body and blood
So that He could give his life for our salvation.

**

Winter time exhibits God's power as trees stripped
and plantings wilted no longer speak of His beauty.
He returns with snow blankets deep that show no partiality
as He gathers His growing's for distant spring grandeur
and summers show of love.

**

Deeper still, will He bob to the
surface, or come round the corner.
The deeper we dig to find Him,
the deeper it seems to get.

**

As loved ones die away and
we are left in loneliness and despair
It's peace to know that You
are here to love us in return.

**

Deep darkness, bottomless black, are You there?
Please shine Your light so I can climb out of this
pit of sorrow and pain.
Why do I love my pain that I don't
give it up for Your love?
What keeps me drawn to blackness when
Your face calls me from this abyss?

**

What measure does He use for Graces given?
Do all the yes's weigh the same to Him?
Do visits to the sick or patience with our fellows
balance the scales like Mary's yes did then?

**

Oh Lord, don't you ever tire of hanging
there because of debtors such as me?
Will You ever say enough to wars or
slaughters done as choice?
We haggle over words when what You long
to hear is I love you and I'll try not to sin again.

**

Our intellect is not enough to lure Him
to appear out of the darkness.
He is not beholden to appear for any human reason,
only with patience and humility can we expect a visit.

**

Oh Blessed Mom who obeyed His plea
to hold His life in you,
Thank you for accepting Him
so we could share Him too.

**

Lord, help me to help them.
I bring Your body to sustain them.
how will they welcome You?
Will it be with a smile or a tear,
I pray it's not a No.
We bear your body to these sick rooms
Yet some deny You and weary You again.
Call me to be your Simon
and bare the weight away.

**

Deeds and frailties which
cannot measure to your
way, teach us Lord

**

How am I to tell of Your wonders when it's taught in silence?
No words come from You, so what words am I to use to tell them?
If they can't see Your word in all creation or in pleading eyes of
    the poor
Then what is left for me to say?

**

So many years the door seemed narrow
for me to wiggle through.
Did my buds refuse to blossom,
Did my seeds forsake to grow?
Lord, shake me from my smugness,
keep me on the path you've planned,
I know I tend to drifting
and ignore my fellow man.
You made us all so we could
come to be like You someday
even the likes of me who tend
to make a mess of things.

**

In silent speak we greet like lovers would
in darkness, You the Day itself.
With graces to disburse,
what will you ask of me this day?
I know you'll ask some tough ones
but you've helped me in the past
to stay on narrow pathways
where the poor and humble plod.

**

I wake from night sleep and find You there, waiting.
Is it because my mind is flushed with troubles settling there?
You must tire of hearing me excuse my way out of them.
I thank the Saints and fools alike who came before and
traveled troubled roads like mine.
Most found the path that You had laid
like this You laid for me.

**

The daisies are hanging on as if they know
what wonders lie behind the Chapel door
that creaks and announces another pilgrim coming in
I should be smiling up too,
indeed for all He lends to me
to give away to some poor soul
who's smiling up at me.

**

We turn our backs on Him,
stirring war pots, raping earth,
killing unborn souls in ever
greater numbers.

**

Even in ancient times, You invited us to your banquets,
and we refused to come over and again.
For millenniums, we've had more
important things to do, we did not come.
If today we hear your voice, will we come,
or will we have more important things to do,
errands to run, or busy killing our neighbors
in the latest war of opportunity, or raping our
environment of it's last vestiges? Or perhaps I'm busy
choosing to let a life live or die in my womb,
or maybe just a quick snort of the latest boutique
drug to get me through my day, or maybe I
have some other banquet of my own to attend that
I've grown fond of in place of yours.
My lifestyle suits me. I like my sin so maybe next time.
Keep in touch, text me any time,
I answer my email when I get a chance.

***

We have nothing to offer Him
that isn't on loan from Him.
What could He do with half a functioning soul
who looks for ways to hide?
That frightens when He calls us up
to do our best for Him?
He's already got lots of slackers who
tend to lesser things, who quit the race
the moment that He needs our best to win.

**

JESUS WHISPER-ER

What mystery, the unseen God
consuming my unseen soul, for Love.

**

Even though Your beauty lies beneath the snow
I heard a dove cry out from barren branches.
Its calling coo's disguised as You in hiding.

**

I thank You for gifts that help me
find You in hidden places.
Don't leave me loose to self,
other lesser gods take your place,
and I'm left alone with me.

**

Jesus whisperers can recognize like souls
those who sing in silent song.
He whispers to us in many ways
in winds that wave the grain
or dance with tree limbs.
Smiles with lips and eyes,
the poor speak like Him to us.
He calls; if only we would answer.

**

Don't let me lag for want of
knowing you.
The fact You came to live and
die is knowledge enough for me.
Just let me seek to find more
love of You each day, to share
the gift with others lost
who can't find love like You.

**

Lord, since silence and darkness is Your home,
Don't let me be wary of seeking You in
souls who cross my path and Your beauty
of creation that sustains us.

**

I wonder if the trees are waiting
for a thawing, buds beneath the bark
prepared to burst.
Are crocus anxious, proud to
show their colors?
All nature seems on hold,
winters had its due.

**

Eyes ask, "What's he want from me?"
smiles tell me 'Thanks' when
offered Holy Gifts.

**

If I am in my prayers
there is less room for
I AM in my soul.
Help me, I AM, to be
self-less, so all
my soul's for You.

**

Lord, when we talk between
ourselves, let it be as two
lovers who long for each other.

**

He came for love that
we could learn to love.
All made alike save
perfect parts like His,
Each uniquely blessed
save one gift all share,
to love His flock
that all were made like Him.

**

Your Beauty blooms in pleading eyes.
asking for Love.
Wake me Lord, I've got enough
to give away your givens.

**

This first day of spring and snow's our only guest.
Trees and bulbs don't seem to mind intrusion,
even robins know new soakings bring worm feasting.
It's humans who tire of winter's traces.
Bring on new buds and blossoms for their like.

**

Here I am Lord, with my wounds, my scars, my nicks.
I'm still in my yesterdays, arguing, attacking, self-ing.
Let me let it be so I can glory in Your today.
Don't let me contaminate it with my me's.

**

Sin is no stranger,
a constant companion.
I'd like to trade it in
and take up Love with You.

**

It's brighter now at seven,
bulbs who slept through winters cold
are breaking though the crust.
Soon their spring clothes will smile up
and show us nature's beauty,
weather not withstanding.

**

Some days, although I'm knocking,
Your answer doesn't come.
You're off with other souls,
those knocking just like me.

**

Three times He appeared to them,
yet they didn't recognize Him.
Even after three years of following.
Times never change, we don't
recognize Him when He passes.
He welcomes us on His terms,
in silence, darkness, and unknowing.

**

Sweet harmony, You and me in love.
Though I can't measure to You,
teach me how to grow.

**

The earth is waiting for Your Beauty to bloom,
much like my soul that seeks You in darkness.

**

Budding trees announce Your presence,
even their branches dance in winds of joy.
Tiny plants work up to spring sun,
grasses grow in celebration too.

**

Spring buds burst upon us,
sleeping all this time in frozen solitude.
They couldn't wait much longer,
holding off from frost and damp and drizzle.
They scream as though to say,
"Enough! we can't hold off another day,
you'll have our beauty all at once."

**

Our landscapes are a-glory, budding.
We're blessed like no others are,
awash in God's beauty showing.
We walk in sleep past others,
who have no treasures such as these.

**

I live in paradox, sick of soul
calling on others sick no less.
bodies warped with pain
seeking Your peace.
They whose limbs and parts need fixing,
me with twisted truth, bent in lust.
Who's less sin-full? I bet He
measured each of us about the same.

**

After Mass he comes, depositing prayer
cards from saints long since removed.
Some complain he bothers silent sessions,
others trade their whispers with him free.
He could be an angel or some other God-ly work.
It's best we be respectful, we beggars
look alike to Him who saves.

**

Have we come full cycle,
Christians fed to beasts
'monst cheering crowds?
Now the fiends hide behind
covered faces;
Christians, pagans too,
slaughtered for their faith.

**

The world is in tumult,
asleep while snakes
slither toward their prey.
The garden suffers which
was made for us.
We wait, wondering when
the venom will reach home.

**

You used a mountainside to
be transfigured in radiant glory.
The whole of creation opened
to this wonderment.
In silence now You offer us this glory.
We need only self as payment in return.
Forgive us Lord when we're busy
chasing lesser Gods we chose.

**

Abba, mold me as clay in potters hands
to become as You in my breath,
my heart, my very soul.

**

 The raw of wilderness speaks in silence,
All we need do is listen for His voice.

**

The trickle of the Baptismal Font,
the beauty of white flowers
staring down from honored places,
proclaim again the wonder of Easter.

**

He's here each day waiting for a visit;
if only we would call.
He's left with empty pews and kneelers
lambs lost, looking for a home.

**

Books for Dummies and How to Do's proliferate.
How to meditate or contemplate,
small group things, prayer groups,
New and Old Testament groups,
all are folly when love
is not the cornerstone.

**

Where are You on dark and
dreary days that hide your beauty?
It's nature that suffers most,
Yet Your lambs still call for You
with weeping eyes hard to hide
in any type of tempest.

**

We pry and snoop but rarely find Him.
He's present though not in full.
He knows that if He shows us all,
we'd wane and wish and whine
for other's gifts to find.

**

Aridity and prayer where God is hidden
in darkness and dryness is a grace He offers,
A space without ourselves where He alone
resides in mystery and love, calling.

**

Your lambs have left for worldly deserts
where evil dwells, tempting them;
shills, offering easy paths to follow
hidden in luring garments
biding for god status in our souls.

**

We know Your lambs who
skitter through the meadows,
new born, leaping, darting,
naïve among the thistles, Satan sown.
May they trend home to mother's
milk that only You provide,
to wise ewes that know the shepherd's
voice that calls, to raise them just for You.

**

Jesus asked them to touch
His wounds and ate with them.
He told them of His fulfillment of old
testimonials, that The Father sent Him
to complete what He had promised;
Eternal life for them.

**

Some of the lilies have drooped
and died but hardy ones remain
much like ourselves,
gatherers at daily Mass.
The blush of Easter missing
now, much like the blooms.
Perhaps some have other things to do.
It's good to see so many recognized
occupying pews they tend to choose.

**

I feel as though I'll burst trying to get it out,
this love that crept up behind to sneak
and fill the damaged holes within my soul.
No other way to explain the words that
float and flow as if by magic pen,
the pens I've used to fill out mostly forms.

**

Faith spurs us to meditate
to try to know the unknowable,
a paradox of dying to selfness,
to live in darkness and silence,
to love Him we've never seen
save times he wishes to share Himself.

**

In darkness and silence, whispers
from yesterdays torment my soul
like busy bodies with nothing to do.
I thought I reached some sort of
bargain with them but they're back
again looking for their due.
I'm tired of their presence, nagging.
My sinfulness causing them to call.

**

Our brains don't balance,
a left that holds our self side
a right dark and deep, a gift
of unknowings holding Spirit.

**

I wish I knew me better,
but much of what I know about me
are secrets hard to share
with others save closest friends.
At what point do I begin to
tell myself the truth and
discover what it is I am?

**

The Niagara River holds Erie water
rushing to becomes Ontario's,
a river 8 miles long, fury infested
waters intimidated by a fall to rocks
now seeking calmer currents hurrying
to the deep of yet another lake.

**

IT'S NOT LIKE SHINING
SHOES

Prayer, and the work that goes into it,
is not like shining shoes; no techniques
handed down, no secrets shared with kin.
No extra elbow grease involved,
there's no right way with it.
You never know the outcome
'cause He's in charge of gifts.

**

Mother Church needs its people to continue
to bring His light to the world, to those
who have retained the truth and to those
brothers and sisters who have strayed
along the way.

**

Holy Mom, whose journey to the manger
was as the Father planned,
you gave birth to Baby Jesus,
as the Father planned.
Our moms gave birth to us in turn
as the Father planned.
Give mothers of today the strength to
pick mangers as He's planned.

**

It was Sunday morning after Mass,
I'm on my way to offer the Eucharist
to souls sick at hospital, bound.
The light is red as she crosses,
Camouflaged and booted, calling
'Where's the light rail?'
'I'm going that way, hop in.'
She volunteered 'Been out all night,
dancing and other things, partyin',
usually I get more than the hundred forty
and they made me clean up the place to boot.'
She acknowledged that she needs to
get a job unlike the one she ply's.
We pulled into the parking lot,
she to hop the train, me to visit His lambs.
I pray I did her right by pointing her to Him.

**

The original twelve were a conglomeration
of mixed up, fearful men,
much like most of us this day.
Each with talents and short-comings
that clashed within the group
(one even failing his mission),
much like most of us this day.
Eleven of twelve got it, finally,
not bad by today's standards,
irony being that The Word's the same
to some of us, as to most that fateful day.

**

The dross is mine,
I let it grow from innocence,
now cluttered with trash
that isn't You, as planned.

**

When I was a tot I learned faith seeded by my father
little did I realize it then.
I recall he had his Bible on the nightstand between their beds.
He knelt down at night at his bed like he taught me to do and
prayed, planting faith seeds in me.
Little did I realize it then.
He was Methodist, raised by his mom's faith seeds,
my mom was Episcopalian, high-type as she liked to say,
more faith seeds sown.
One of my great grandfathers came from Europe and bought
some land and built a church still standing 'til this day; more seeds.
My faith was seeded broad but thin but others came along,
Desert Fathers and Mothers, even Popes, Bishops,
Kings and beggars, friends, enemies, most were lovers,
saints great and small planting other seeds.
The more I've been seeded the less I seem to know about
the great mysteries of my faith.
But I know there more seeds coming if I just make ground for them.

**

He wasn't recognizable on the road to
Emmaus 'til He decided so.
He opened the fellow travelers' eyes at
table when He proclaimed His body
and blood as food.
His fellow travelers lost sight of Him
The same as when we leave Him in
the Monstrance at the chapel all alone.

**

Sometimes they wake you up early in their searching and buzzing, you had to swat them if you wanted any peace, rolled up paper would do but you usually missed most swipes 'til at last you squashed them on the wall.

Like most uninvited guests, flies know how to get in, any hole will do, even easy entry thru open windows and screen doors.

We tried to keep them out, but busted screens were their
 companions.

Some folks had swatters, better than rolled up papers; older family, grammas and grampas, had great wrist action and could hit the buggers in mid-air.

We youngins would borrow their swatters but olders didn't want
 you messin'
with their equipment, especially when you didn't put it back.

Now we have thermal windows and doors, flies need more creativ-
 ity now and
search for openings. We have sprays and traps now, we're locked
 in our
cocoons of media controlled environment. To Google is to know
 now-days
but it doesn't raise the juices like a good battle with the acrobatic fly,
 one on one, no holds barred.

**

It was part of one of those precious moments
when you meet Him in one of your brothers
who had met Him in the death of his daughter.
It's an experience that contemplative souls have,
if at all, when they're blessed with His presence,
yet so difficult to put into words; one of those
moments when it's a witness of His Spirit with you.
His daughter went through a long period of suffering,
times she wished to remain private, remaining strong
within her faith that all would come to pass, the
strongest of those around her, just as God had planned.
Her memory lives on in those who remain, it's to their
benefit that they met one of His lovers such as she.

**

All creation is good because
You created it from nothing.
We misuse your creation
when we waste it
or worship it in place of You.

✻✻

I want to follow where You lead me,
Does it mean I must come up with plans?
Is there some form I need or password to let me in?
Is there experience I need or a resume of some kind?
What school would help, whose name to drop,
could You take me as I am with all my scars and bruises?
Aren't You used to my excuses or the plans that never work?
I won't use my old ideas or words all hollowed out.
I'll just wait for tender mercies and love I've known before
to pick me up and whole me and set me on my feet.

✻✻

It's still dark at morning rising,
what will the weather be
per chance it's sun we're looking for
or will clouds hold back Your beauty?
The poor and un-homed have passed the night,
what rags and cardboard sheltered them?
They'll be harder to find today, hunkered down
with smelly clothes still dank from yesterdays.
I wonder if they'll think of me as I have thought of them?
There's not much they can do for me that You haven't already
    done,
but You keep bringing up their plight that haunts me,
where are they, what are they doing, what shape are they in,
what gender, what color skin, what age?
You don't count the cards like this when handing out Your love to
    me.
Why do I not do the same, You made them just like me?

✻✻

A poor prairie farmer from the Dakotas and
his pregnant wife visited the Windy City
for some rest and recreation.
Most rooms were taken, they settled for cheap rates.
They no sooner checked in, then labor pains
announced the arrival of their first born, a son.
After a couple days rest, a knock on the door announced
arrival of three prominent investors bearing gifts
enough for the new parents to think about returning home
to start their own enterprise. They crept out the back way
hordes of press, gossip columnists, Hollywood admirers,
even a politico or two, and 6-8-11 news anchors.
The little family became one of the world's latest billionaires
with oceans of oil below their modest farmstead.

**

If we seek to find Him we usually never do.
Mostly we see His face in others.
He'll surprise us when we least expect Him.
It's most times when we persevere in humility
that He will surprise us with wonder.

**

Some are offered suffering as a wake-up
call from the Beloved, a sentinel reminding
us that our earthly time is nearing a close.
If we have asked to discern your will then
we must be alert, suffering may be the sign
He has prepared for us.

**

Contrast the above with a young girl from a village
called Nazareth just wanting to be counted as ordered,
along with her carpenter-husband and unborn child.
They had a devil of a time getting reasonable shelter
so they settled on a manger to lie in of all things,
complete with animals and hay, smells included.
No sooner were they at rest when a Child was born,
whose treasure was deeper and longer lasting
than anyone could imagine, everlasting redemption for all!
The little group received three callers, Kings with gifts,
but no other fanfare was recorded.
The three guests, along with the lowly girl, her husband
and the newborn had to sneak out of town to escape
a crazy man who felt frightened by their presence.

**

You replace with You what You take from us,
exchanges lovingly made,
at once perhaps a loved one or some malady for us.
We're weakened souls, but graces are given to replace our voids,
in return be strong, persistent in our chase,
feeble as we have become, we're not in competition,
to balance scales or bid ones side to win.

**

When I look for you and you
choose to hide your face,
give me patience to seek and
find you, with me bearing my
cross as Simon did for you.

**

God's winter beauty is simpler to discern
than other seasons He has created;
the spring with it's fresh beginnings,
the summer with it's endless bounty,
the fall with the last gasps of farewell colors.
Winter dress does not give as much distinction
as others, it's blanket of snow is all there is to see.
The trees seem to tell the snow to fall where leaves last
graced it's limbs or lie below and nourish roots
and wait to melt, to water springs arrival soon.

**

Your seeds still grow,
even in our stubbornness and impatience.
It's us who don't cooperate, busy with our
gods we're reluctant to release.

**

Heavenly Word, I must give up any concepts
or descriptions of you, for what is known of your totality,
or what Saint has been able to tell it or give it human forms
of meaning. Faith is your holder if in fact you can be held.
We know of no shape of you; does spirit have fullness or
is it a state of being that only you can choose to share with us?
What will we become in the after life, can we expect to see each
other as we see each now, in our purification will we be angel like?

**

It's a cold and damp day upon us,
Your beauty hidden in misty rain,
ice formed under foot.
My joy is in knowing that
in Your love and mercy,
though hidden in wintry weather,
You're always lurking, soul ward watching,
waiting in wonderment for me to call again.

**

Lord, I pray for 'especiallies', sheep
both sick or wounded, wandering.
Some have asked for prayers for help for
those with outward wounds, others with
inner pains that grew from evil seeds
Some are lonely; those whose spouse has passed,
or those with closest friends no more,
who took wrong forks on roads,
and seek their way back home.
Some who just seem lost and bowed,
hunched from heavy loads,
who need a hand like Simon
showed for Christ so long ago.

**

Oh gracious God what mystery that you remember me
though countless other souls have come before.
You love us same as them though we are but blowing dust.
I pray you make me as an oak with roots to match
So when your wind gives rise, I won't scatter as I'm prone.

**

It wasn't pain that held me,
She caught me without patience.
And I treated her with disdain on
bothering me as to how to clean
the refrigerator door or other messes
I continually leave for her to clean.
Help me to be more Mary and less Martha
When it comes to daily chores.
That I honor her wishes in how to raise
the child in me that I thought I had outgrown.

**

You have long labored in His vineyard
as a faithful servant.
He found you there and took his place in
the secret of your soul.
Your next calling is another blessing
giving you more time to be alone with
the Beloved.
Now less interlopers of your time,
those who benefited by your Pastoral witness.
Retirement will be more like a retreat,
when He gives you your wages for a job
well done, but never over.

**

In Your plan, do You have certain souls
picked out that I am You to them?
What if I miss one in my day,
do You excuse my fault?
There are so many lost in life.
I can always find a soul
who seeks to see Your eyes
of light in others weak like me.

**

Though we talk in secret silence, unnoticed,
give me purpose to share
Your love with other laborers,
hidden in their response 'to follow Me'.
Not only to follow, but to become.

**

Pieces of Your puzzle arrive to kneel in silence,
eyes open looking at Your body hanging there,
others with head bowed down, no less in love.

**

We are poor, no less than street poor
quaking in bread lines.
Our hunger is for the Bread promised
to fill our soul, holes we've
prepared for You to come to rest awhile.

**

We are seeds you have sown in Eternal time.
Are we growing straight or have we dried?
Are we crooked or have we stretched to the sun?
Did our roots mature as planned so we could pod?
Have we grown our seeds you have loaned
us to cast for You?
Seeds sown over all these years,
how many I wasted on other gods.
Many bloomed to beauty but wilted
away un-watered.
What waste I wrought in haste,
seeking other gods.

**

We can't expect to find you when we like.
It's up to You when You decide the play.
Besides silence and darkness,
You may plan a poor beggars eyes to suffice.

**

Each day dawns and You become my
interest like a lover would.
What am I to say, is it enough
to repeat words we've exchanged
or are You growing tired
of emptiness from me?

**

Seeds flow from His Body as we partake
of Him as He commanded us.
The seeds grow and bind us to His Church
A holy reciprocity ensues, love exchanged.

**

Jesus, may my soul be cleansed
deep within it's clefts and crannies.
Where You hide, a place we share in secret,
only You and I know of it; swept and scrubbed
so nothing save love is shared there.
What began as a command has grown into
blissful habit, love begetting love.
You offered a pact, to love You and our neighbors
alike, as we love ourselves, a sacred charge indeed.

**

Help me to remember when
at times I am fearful and faithless,
that you are resting in the bow,
ready to calm the turbulence around me,
if only I bid you.
Remind me how your love can overcome
the evil one vying for my soul.

**

Lord, may I always seek you in others,
exchanging your grace,
accepting them in their space.

**

Simeon and Anna recognized
the savior in baby form.
We are blessed to recognize
His spiritual form in the faces
of the poor and down trodden.

**

I made my usual rounds calling on
the sick and broken but I did not
recognize Your face in them.
Was it me who didn't look for You
or were You hiding there all alone?
I have no right to think You're waiting
for me though I'm sick and broken too.

**

While You were with us You cured Jairus'
daughter and the hemorrhaging woman,
telling witnesses not to tell anyone,
Faith in You was their reward that You
would do such things.
Praise was not of your concern
but your love would be the prize.

**

In a boat on the lake
on the side of a mountain,
out in the waste of the desert,
were they your secret-silent
time with the Father?
Our silence is consumed
by lesser gods barking their wares,
shouting their empty promises.
We seem trapped in this luring,
ultimately to die for it.
May You continue your
presence in our secret silence,
public expressions of your mercy
in the begging eyes of the poor.

**

O Love, hiding in soul's clefts and crannies,
waiting for a visit,
You go out with me into the world,
Searching for lovers.
Your love and mercy are our wages,
Given bountifully, to even such as me.

**

As we begin, You and I,
sort me out Lord
that I might best follow.
Challenge me, for I tend
to sluff-ness and laze.
I pray our goal is love,
love that's new, that draws
me on, deep, closer,
ever closer, more like You,
less like me.

**

When I was young, my soul
seemed purer, but my energy
level was high, a wrong turn here,
a missed opportunity there,
treading where I shouldn't,
in innocence I didn't know the wrongs.
I'm over 80 now, scars abound, nicks
that sting and hurt from stumbles earned.
I pray when called I'll be more like
when I was mostly free from self
and worldly ways.

**

Today, the gift You gave me,
My love who shares my life,
is one year round again.
We seem to know each other's play
better than our own.
She is best for me when I
am cool and rightly should be hot,
she settles me to see a better way.
Thank You Lord, that Your plan
for me was her, may I be plans for her.

**

Oh faith that holds your dark mysteries
what am I to expect to witness
in my soul's secret places?
How will I recognize what is
offered me to behold?
Your saints past had no words
to describe you.
If they were wanting, how
do you expect a sinner such
as me to respond?
But then, all things are possible
with You.

**

How to compete with technology
when quick solutions in less time
are the goal.
It would be a reasonable trade-off
if the time saved could be traded for
time used in silence and answers
that don't respond to quick time,
some answers seem destined
to take a lifetime.

**

The barbarians are loose, raping,
killing, beheading, destroying;
even their own are fair game.
It seems the world's on fire,
who and what is to be saved,
left to warrant love and mercy?
The barbarians have no sacred-ness
about them; all are privy to their wrath.
Their targets earn no place in honors circle,
we too are lost, life itself is cheap.
We take to killing in the womb,
millions suffer slaughter there,
death meets them in their mother's
womb before they witness lives
that You had planned.
You must be sad, You lived and
died to save us all and we have come
full cycle, back to Golgotha's shame.

**

To know Him only in the intellect
Which ignores the gentle blush that
accompanies an emotional attachment.

**

It's scarily quiet, no nuisance noises
to blame for wandering minds.
The Tabernacle holds its precious secret,
it doesn't need any added brilliance,
stained glass windows look the same as past.
Pews seem relaxed waiting for guests
it must be me that causes interruptions,
perhaps He's glad to have my visit.

**

Oh Lord, in our silent visits
don't let me be haughty
expecting more than planned.
What you have given to me
may be all there is to give.
Was some other seed sown
that wasn't meant for me,
or did you tire of waiting
for a yes that you'd expect?
Scraps from your table
would satisfy my needs,
other tender morsels
you've given in the past
were wasted in my dallying.

**

As long as there is wind you're with us,
bright sun that shows off your beauty
in bending trees whose limbs seem to
dance with joy to have you round.

**

He is the word and the light and the truth
and the salvation in infinitude.
The closer I get to Him the further
I must travel, I shall never know it all,
that's left for eternity to blossom.

**

Breathe on me Lord, I woke without it;
worries streaked through me
places I didn't want to be, deserts
where beasts breathing took Your place.
Breathe on me Lord, bring me back to You

**

Where and how will I trend today,
will I be hot or cold, will I see Him
at Mass or will I miss Him in
distractions, maybe in the parking
lot, but then I need to beat the traffic
out to work and it's possibilities in
other tribal things or going home where
patience and humility suffer; other fools
like me hurry to mix with families woes
but I'm aloof, I have problems too,
another wasted day on finite things.

**

I thank you for this day that I can be You
in all I do or say, in all I love and pray,
today has possibilities for mercy and
thanksgiving, yesterdays are done.
I hope I measured up though I know I
never do, tomorrow merits some concern,
let me leave alone what You have planned,
so I can give my best for today's, full heed.

**

When You display the wind in all it's fury
man's created things get broken, twisted, or
drift away, yet there are those who over look
the Spirit that You brought that gifted us with
raw materials to play the games of god's.

**

I was staring at the warped wooden fence that
man had made, dwarfed by the majestic pine
disfigured of limbs where once these timbers grew.

**

Why can't I commit to sin no more?
My love is not enough it seems.
Others past have loved enough to
purify their lives, it grieves me Lord
that I can't do the same.
Help me to rise above myself
so I can give you all and be
what You have planned.

**

I know I search in secret places
but what I bring does not unlock the door.
.My knock is weak for conscience reigns,
I don't merit spaces blessed by You.

**

You wept in the final hours of human life,
not for self but for sinners such as me.
How often must You have wept since then.
I've often let You down and
nailed You back again.

**

They peer out from deserts of their own making
poor in spirit sick in beds or corners rushing
some with just their tears or cardboard signs
food and jobs make up their lists
when mostly love and mercy is their cure.

**

SILENT SPEAK

I thank You for this day that I can be You
in all I do or say, in all I love and pray.
today has possibilities for mercy and
thanksgiving, yesterdays are done.
I hope I measured up though I know
I never do, tomorrow merits some concern.
let me leave alone what You have planned,
so I can give my best to You today.

**

Oh faith, that holds Your dark mysteries,
what am I to expect to witness
in my soul's secret places?
How will I recognize what is
offered me to behold?
Your saints past had no words
to describe You.
If they were wanting, how
do You expect a sinner such
as me to respond?
But then, all things are possible
with You.

**

Oh Lord, where have I been where You have been, all along?
While I was wallowing and struggling, caught up in me,
you were watching and waiting in patient silence for my return.
Only by Your grace have I survived 'til now,
roughed up and scraped, out of step most times,
an accident waiting to happen though You chose
to save me, always, again.

**

Oh Love, hiding in souls clefts
and crannies, waiting for a visit,
You go out into the world.
searching for lovers.
Your love and mercy are our wages,
given bountifully, to even such as me,

**

As we begin, You and I,
sort me out Lord
that I might best follow.
Challenge me, for I tend
to sluff-ness and laze.
I pray our goal is Love,
Love that's new, that draws
me on, deeper, closer.
ever closer, more like You,
less like me.

**

All Beauty is from You.
May I discern it in all I see today.
Don't allow me to overlook Your
presence when man's ugliness
screams at me to look.

**

How to compete with technology
when quick solutions in less
time is the goal.
It would be a reasonable trade-off
if the time saved could be swapped
for time used in silence and answers
that don't respond to quick time,
Some answers seem destined
to take a lifetime.
He is the Word and The Light
and The truth, the salvation in infinitude.
The closer I get to Him the further
I must travel, I shall never know it all,
that's left for eternity to blossom.

**

While You were with them, You cured Jarius's
daughter and a hemorrhaging women
instructing witnesses not to tell anyone.
Faith in You was their reward that You
could do such things.
Praise was not Your concern,
Your Love would be the reward.

**

When I look for You and You
choose to hide Your face,
give me patience to seek and
find You, with me bearing
my cross as Simon did for You.

**

What mystery, the unseen God
consuming my unseen soul, for Love.

**

If we seek to find Him we usually never do,
mostly we see His face in others.
He'll surprise us when we least expect Him.
It's most times when we persevere in humility
that He will surprise us with His wonderment.

**

Deeper still will He bob to the
surface or come round the corner.
The deeper we dig to find Him
the deeper it seems to get.

**

Why not be born in a stable where the poor and animals live?
After all His mom was a peasant girl and His step dad a
    tradesman.
The child's mission was to die and save the lowly and the poor,
not just Kings like those who offered first gifts to Him.
Strips of cloth were manger wear for this Son of God
who arrived in Bethlehem in His naked humanity,
No in-laws to gift a crib or car seat,
The Christ child left town in Mary's arms on donkey back
led toward Egypt by Joseph to escape a crazy king.

**

Deeds and frailties which
don't measure to Your
way, teach us Lord.
Day begins with petitions, where do we begin?
From Your first gift of life, where do we start?
How does one count the beach-sands or the
waves that pound them there?
We overlook most blessings, forgive us Lord
that I withhold my love in rare thanks-giving.

**

Oh Lord, don't You ever tire of hanging
there because of debtors such as me/
Will You ever say enough to wars
or slaughters done in name of choice?
We haggle over words when what You long
to hear is I Love You and I'll try not to sin again?

**

Why can't I commit to sin no more,
my love is not enough it seems.
Others past have loved enough to
purify their lives,
it grieves me Lord,
that I can't do the same.
Help me to rise above myself
so I can give you all and be
what You have planned for me.

**

He came to live and die
not just for His age but all mankind
He taught us to live and die to self.
His seeds sown to branch to oaken strength,
Not like seeds sown by evil kings
That sprout as weeds and choke
out weaken growth
Oh Timeless One, another day You've
given, to live and seek and love.
What again will I complicate, when plain
it's me You seek.

**

If God is for me, who can be against me?
Surely, not the me that's made like me
but the me that's made like You.

**

Oh Blessed Mom who
obeyed His plea
to hold His life in you
thank you for accepting Him
so we could share Him too.

**

Oh Perfect Sacrifice, what little we in turn
give back to You in love.
The pursuit is never ending and Your
promise drives me on.

**

Abraham, forerunner of Him who gave
His Son for love, so it was with you.
What faith it took to leave your home
to climb the mount, to raise the knife,
If I'd been called, I'd still be home,
bartering with no leverage, save
some small exchanges with the poor.

**

Our soul is His temple and we must
be diligent, no dross or clutter find,
Just a place for Him to rest
and show His Beauty there.

**

God is The Word and The Word
became flesh to dwell amongst us
No sin does He bear, no imperfections,
Fully human, fully divine,
no foolishness, no weaknesses.

**

Lord, since silence in darkness is Your home,
don't let me wary of seeking You in souls
who cross my path bearing the beauty
of Your creation that sustains me.

**

He created us to be Him to each other,
loving and kind, self-less,
merciful without guile,
each given a human stint,
earthly time to fall in love with Him
with mercy and forgiveness
second chances do abound
will He tire and say enough,
send us off to Babylon and
destroy Jerusalem again?

**

Each moment is opportunity and encounter,
one of His moments given to us
All is His love, none is our self-love
His to exchange with other lovers,

**

Don't let me lag for want of
knowing You
The fact You came to live and
die is know enough for me
Just let me seek to find more
love of You each day to share
the gift with others lost
who can't find love like You.

**

Though You hide in darkness waiting,
open my eyes to Your beauty offered
for my taking.

**

I thank You for gifts that help me
find You in hidden places
don't let me loose to self,
other, lesser gods take Your place
and I'm left alone with me.

**

Greeks and pagans came to meet Him.
He was there to touch and see, teaching among them,
His presence a small part of all His nature.
In our age we look to find Him still, but mostly
never see Him in other eyes that plead
'cause we haven't learned to see His beauty
in those who make up most of what we do,
at home and Church and work and play
and spaces in between, where He has taken up
with poor and needy souls as me.

**

On our high mountains, deserts too, we
witness You as Your priest prays
for bread and wine to become
Your living self, what wonderment!
On Your high mountain, Saints shared
a mystery, Transfiguration, God clouded.
They were told to tell not a soul.
we too must leave with our instruct
to be transfigured, but to share the good news.

**

The Divine Master possesses all things in creation and
shares all of it in love with His laborers in the field.
We are not to pick and chose among His gifts like children in
a candy store, nor pout and stomp our feet when others have more
    toys.
We are not to nibble at others goods as if we deserved a share
If we accept His gifts and offer them to others who are without.
we do His will and please Him in return.

**

Who or where would I be
without Your forgiveness?

**

They peer out from deserts of their own making
poor in spirit, sick in beds or corners begging,
some with just their tears or cardboard signs
food and jobs make up their lists
when mostly love and mercy is their cure.

**

When I was young, my soul
seemed purer, energy level
high, a wrong turn here a
missed opportunity there,
treading where I shouldn't,
innocence, I didn't know the wrongs.
I'm older now, scars abound, nicks
that sting and hurts from stumbles taken
I pray when called I'll be more like
I was, mostly free from self
and worldly things.

**

To know Him only with the intellect
ignores the gentle blush that
accompanies an emotional attachment.
There once was a young girl from a village
called Nazareth just wanting to be counted as ordered
along with her carpenter-husband and unborn Child.
They had a devil of a time getting reasonable shelter
so they settled on a manger to lie in of all things,
complete with animals and hay, smells included.
No sooner were they at rest when the Child was born
whose coming meant more than anyone could imagine,
everlasting redemption for all.
The little group received three callers, Kings with gifts,
no other fanfare was recorded.
The three guests departed, along with the lowly girl,
her husband and the new born, sneaking out of town to escape
a crazy man who felt threatened by their presence.

**

Your beauty blooms in pleading
eyes asking for love.
Wake me Lord, I've got enough
to give away that you have given me.

**

No one shares our silent place
where I pine to meet You,
a place where our words are
never given away, where mostly
I listen more than speak,
For what am I to say that You
don't already know?

**

Let me see Your lambs
not with my eyes but Yours.

**

If You are in all, let me see You in all,
both the beauty that is Yours and
the lesser things that man owns.

**

Lord, I give You my day.
Any good I do is You,
forgive me when I give
what's me.

**

The contemplative life leads us deeper
into the mystery of God.
As we plunge deeper into mystery
we come to know less about Him
whom we are seeking.
We never arrive closer to answers,
only that we come up with more questions.
The intellect starves as faith fattens on the mystery.

**

Light of Love, probe my soul,
drive out lingering darkness
Lead me back to Jerusalem to
the hill of shame where I can
meditate on Your love and light.
Forgive my sins and lies that nail
You back upon the tree.
Turn on Your light so I can see
You sitting in the pews all round me.

**

Good Shepard, Your lambs have strayed
down into deep gullies and washes,
down where wolves wait, hungry.
You hurry after them, Your sashes flying.
Your willing to die for them, even to hang on a tree.
What price to pay for wanderers such as we,
We'll be off again and You'll be right behind
to anoint our heads and overflow our cups.

**

Our prodigal sons and daughters,
how do we welcome there return?,
what inheritance have we left them
to help them deal with our tarnished world,
the many pigsties to work and corn husks to eat.
I see many of them coming down the road,
let us welcome them home with God-like love
that was denied them in their youth while we
pursued our fortunes of folly.
After all, we told them the future was plastics.

**

Easter lasts through smiling daisy faces
looking out in awe at what they've seen
A Man was killed upon a cross who wasn't due it
then slept three days and rose for all
as He promised He would do.
Now what are we to offer Him in trade?

**

Silence and solitude suffer from the
mechanical and technical onslaught
of the latest electronic must haves.
We no longer listen to our inner voice
but prefer the persistent clamor of hawkers.

**

Whose shoes are we to walk in before we know?
Who was Freddie Gray or each of 6 who chased him?
And who and what am I, or all of Baltimore?
How can I judge another when I'm lame at judging me?
So much noise surrounds us and most not listening worth.
Do we all live in confusion, are we afraid of truth?
We're angry at each other, we differ in our pick.
our friends, our groups, our gods and devils same.
We love our addictions and hates we've sown
in lifetimes filled with words of media frenzy
that sway our judgment and skew our views.

**

Who is anyone when most we know are externals,
We don't know the full where the deep mind rules
the spirit place where our being lies
We search to know Him there, never closer,
always darker, all in silence.

**

It seems a miracle, the crash
this burst upon my soul
You speak to me in deep
pains suffered, yet not suffered
the harsh roughness of rehab
yet not harsh or rough
I can't imagine You need me Lord
yet it's hard to see why you've spared
me much worst cripplings set before me
have I been picked to help You
In some way?

**

Without You by I'm like a small child
stumbling through a maze of human make
that tries to lead me off the path You chose
most times I've failed when led my lowly louts

**

He visits us when we meet Him in the smiles
and tears of others same as we.
broken and rubbed by life we chose to lead.
If only we would stick to narrow gates
that lead to Transfiguration as his Son
displayed on a desert mountain side.

**

7AM MASS-24 HR.CHAPEL

Your legions are arriving, each peers to see who shares the pews,
are they regulars or is this someone new there?
Heads down or up, some frowns and smiles a-mix.
It's comfort to the regulars to see new faces there
'cause it pleases Him who comes to visit too.

**

It's quiet, only early souls are here.
A distant voice is out beyond the door.
It's one of us who comes with wife in tow.
She's sweet and smiles but never kneels or
walks the aisle to bliss and beauty, The Eucharist.
when Mass concludes, he leads her out to home
with her smile in place.

**

It's middle fall and semi-darkness, Mass is calling.
Some cars, Paul's and Phil's and Frank's.
They have their spots along with the silent one
who never speaks and leaves alone for work.
I know most all by name if not by back of head.
What brings them here each day like me?
It's not for me to know, those too in search of mystery,
fully revealed. I offer prayers for what they pray for.
Like me, can they discern His will that He has planned for them?

**

This wall, these windows, the altar, flowers, Tabernacle,
candles, the remaining souls in pews about.
You're everywhere, in sunlight streaming in,
the very life you give to breath, I need not search afar.

**

Most hustle out, urgencies calling,
others huddle in little groups, whispering,
A few kneel or sit in silence in private prayers.
Which do You prefer, or does any recognition
prove enough to lighten Your Cross,
carrying our sins about?
What can we do to make up for the times
we pass You by and fail to kiss Your wounds?

**

This life, this world, this very day would be naught,
save faith and prayer in You.
Who could we believe in or petition for our needs?
My step outside my door each day would lack
it's wonder, the road to Emmaus would not
include other journeymen.
The Church would be darkened, no others,
no Mass to glory in.
You wouldn't be there to welcome us with Love.

**

Oh precious silence when candles die and voices fade away.
The Mass is over but You remain hidden in darkness
behind Tabernacle doors.
It's time to leave and find You waiting on the street.
I know You're there in eyes that weep for love.
I search for You in other faces
and mostly find You there, exchanged.

**

Help me to overcome self today in all I do, in all I see.
In all I meet, in all I love, as if it's the first we've ever met.
May I live and love in truth of whom and what I am
and how little that sums up to be when excluding You.

**

Though You are unknown in darkness, Your presence
is palpable when sitting in a pew, silent with other pilgrims.
Prayers arrive and sit in their private pew spaces
as if they're like pieces fitting in a puzzle.

**

I marvel as the 'early's' adore You in silence,
it lifts my soul with them.
Wordless praise, what glories pass their tongues?
You listen to them all.
The 'fronts' and 'backs' have now arrived,
they seem to save 'middle pews' for later souls
Most hire to harvest too, their wages same as ours,
no need to measure them.
The mass is o're, and each soul has their parting,
some rush out to fill a schedule self imposed,
others talk aloud about last nights win or loss,
some leaving seem to sense that quiet worked for them.
A small and dwindling few need more time and so
remain in silence off alone with Him.
As we leave this Holy place we must remember to take our
souls along, His sheep await us to help them home again.

**

Decorations down, wreaths and boughs away 'til Advent next.
Your Beauty lasts among the altar blooms
And 'hind Tabernacle doors waiting in darkness and silence
As You did in deserts and on mountain sides,
Praying for un-worthies in Your midst like me.

**

Pieces of Your puzzle arrive to kneel in silence,
Eyes open looking at Your Body hanging there.
others with heads bowed down, no less in love.

**

I missed the last few days at Mass
The hole in my soul was larger than expected,
growing there for lack of seeing You.
Names returned as each went up the aisle,
familiar coughs popped up as if by clue.
Each took their favorite space that they took owner of.
The Lector same and Priest I knew,
No different than last I came.
The Mass was o're and I felt back at home.

**

The Virgin was called
and gave a yes,
To grow the Christ bound
by her body and blood,
so that He could give His life
for our salvation.

**

Ice does not deter them all
Just some who rightly miss
others come, go through their rites
bowing, kneeling, sitting,
staring silence, greeting Love
waiting 'hind Tabernacle doors.

**

It's scary quiet, no nuisance noise
to blame for wandering minds.
The Tabernacle holds it's precious gift,
It doesn't need any added glory,
stained glass windows look the same as past,
pews seem wanting waiting for guests
It must be me that causes interruption,
though I know He's glad to have a visit.

**

Oh Chapels banging door and furnace fan,
creaking hinge, all break the spell.
Call me home to You.

**

It's deep into winter and no one visits.
Old buddies at home holed up against the cold.
It's boring not having them about
I'm idled peeling back the husks
That bind a soul filled with clutter from
a life of wasted times that could have been used
to find You hidden in the poor that passed
by without a helping hand from me.

**

He's a quiet man, tall, erect, silent, hardly speaking.
He marches upright to the front, kneeling the same.
Dan's the name and I replied I'm Bill,
But since that day he's never used my name again
Until one frigid day when he, in front, held the
door for me, I called his name again,
He spoke aloud 'I've forgotten yours'
At last He shared himself with me.

**

In the quiet of The Chapel
You plant Your seeds in silence.
Other pilgrims come and go.
It's winter, the air filled with
furnace noise and coughs
A soul comes in, breathless in distress.

**

You're all alone, empty seats,
No silent conversations going forth.
I'm sure You grieve when
You're alone like this,
no souls in thanksgiving,
no hopefuls kneeling down,
no one needing healing.
You're there in front, Monstrance bound,
If only we would call.

**

The Chapel's neatly kept, The Monstrance beckoning
Peace is palpable interrupted by other sinners calling.
As I sit before The monstrance, I wonder what He sees in me.
In silence different guests arrive who interrupt the peace
and mostly interfere and block His view for me.
The Master knows this well, there's no rush, no
competition or timing, you'll find Him when
He's ready, keep alert, simple and poor in spirit.
I often fail to find Him in haughty places,
Why surf the internet or seek Him in the media
It's fruitless to find His majesty there.
He's always silently sitting here waiting for a kiss.

**

He wasn't recognized on the road to Emmaus
until He decided so.
He opened the fellow travelers eyes at
table when He proclaimed His body
And blood as food.
His fellow travelers lost sight of Him
The same as when we leave Him in
The Monstrance at the Chapel all alone.

**

Sitting before The Monstrance,
my soul fills up for the Beloved
I sense He's happy we're visiting
Will I be able to retain His graces
storing up within my soul
or will I burst and deflate like a child's balloon?
I pray I can hold graces long enough to give
them to the poor I meet begging for Your Love.

**

ABOUT THE AUTHOR

   Bill Phillips was born in 1931 in Niagara Falls, NY, son of
Protestant parents. The family moved to Maryland in 1932, Denver
in 1942, and back to Maryland after WWII. He was educated in
public and private schools until entering Loyola College in 1951.
He converted to Catholicism in 1952 and graduated in 1955. Bill
is married to Pat, has five children and 13 grandchildren. He
retired in 2010 as a senior residential appraiser and member of the
appraisal institute. He resides with Pat in Cockeysville, MD.

Apprentice House is the country's only campus-based, student-staffed book publishing company. Directed by professors and industry professionals, it is a nonprofit activity of the Communication Department at Loyola University Maryland.

Using state-of-the-art technology and an experiential learning model of education, Apprentice House publishes books in untraditional ways. This dual responsibility as publishers and educators creates an unprecedented collaborative environment among faculty and students, while teaching tomorrow's editors, designers, and marketers.

Outside of class, progress on book projects is carried forth by the AH Book Publishing Club, a co-curricular campus organization supported by Loyola University Maryland's Office of Student Activities.

Eclectic and provocative, Apprentice House titles intend to entertain as well as spark dialogue on a variety of topics. Financial contributions to sustain the press' work are welcomed. Contributions are tax deductible to the fullest extent allowed by the IRS.

To learn more about Apprentice House books or to obtain submission guidelines, please visit www.apprenticehouse.com.

Apprentice House
Communication Department
Loyola University Maryland
4501 N. Charles Street
Baltimore, MD 21210
Ph: 410-617-5265 • Fax: 410-617-2198
info@apprenticehouse.com • www.apprenticehouse.com

CPSIA information can be obtained at www.ICGtesting.com
Printed in the USA
BVOW08s0814070816

457914BV00003B/12/P